ALL TOLEDO

Text, photographs, diagrams and reproduction conceived and carried out in their entirety by the technical teams of EDITORIAL ESCUDO DE ORO, S.A.

Rights on reproduction and translation (whole or part) reserved.

Copyright of photographs and literary text of the present edition:
© EDITORIAL ESCUDO DE ORO, S.A.
Palaudàries, 26 - 08004 Barcelona (Spain)

© EL GRECO, «The Burial of the Count of Orgaz» (1586-1588)
Parish Church of Santo Tomé. Toledo. Spain.

Editorial Escudo de Oro, S.A.

Aerial view of Toledo.

INTRODUCTION: the historical background and urban development of Toledo

The visitor arrives in Toledo to see a fortified city on an ochre mountain, bathed in sunlight and encircled and besieged by the Tagus River, which flows determinedly around the hillside. In order to take in the city in its entirety, before you enter the maze of narrow streets and the complexity of its long history, admire it from the other side of the impressive canyon formed by the Tagus River as it passes by Toledo by taking the ringroad set with vantage points that offer the most spectacular panoramic views of the city. From the vantage point next to the Shrine of the Virgen del Valle, or from behind the Rock of the Moorish King of legend, or from the National Parador hotel, you can see the emblematic architectural skyline of Toledo: the motley of brown buildings with the Alcázar (fortress) and Cathedral rising above them, and with the stylised silhouette of the many Mudejar towers doing battle with the great dome of the Church of San Juan de los Reyes. The city is, in short, a body of architectural monuments constructed over different periods –justly appreciated by UNESCO, which declared Toledo a World Heritage Site in 1987– which make the old city centre a veritable city-museum.

As a true reflection of its glorious past, the city on the Tagus presents the unmistakable face of the Middle Ages, when it rose to become one of the most important and influential cultural centres in the world. This is what is known as «Toledo of the Three Cultures», a period when Jews, Muslims and Christians lived culturally and religiously side by side; a period which began in the 8th century, after the Arab invasion of the city, spanning the time when the city fell finally into Christian hands in 1085 and which stretched through to the end of the 15th century, when it was decreed that the Jews be expelled in 1492, followed by the Mudejars in 1502. Mudejar art, the style which so characterises the city, was the fruit of this cultural co-existence. However, Toledo had already blossomed as the capital of the Visigothic monarchy and as the seat of the well-known Councils of Toledo. The city was also later to be one of the most active focal points of the Spanish Renaissance and its name is closely linked to that of El Greco. It must not be forgotten, as various authors have already stated,

that Toledo in itself is a microcosm of the history of Spain as a whole.

Its strategic location in the centre of the Iberian peninsula on a rocky promontory (stretching 1.5 km long and 1 km wide), which runs alongside the Tagus River, making it an impregnable site, has been a decisive factor in the city's history. It is known that there was an important emplacement here in the area, known as Carpetania during the Celtiberian period. In 192 BC, this enclave was taken by the legions of Marcus Fulvius Nobilior. Its name was changed to Toletum and it became a key place for dominating the Tagus. There are few remains left from the Roman

View of the old centre from the Rock of the Moorish King.

Ruins of the Roman Circus from La Vega Baja.

period, but these reveal that it was a sizeable city as it had an amphitheatre (situated according to research in the Las Covachuelas neighbourhood) and a circus that could seat over 30,000 spectators (the ruins can be seen in Vega Baja). The Romans also put up the first stretch of city walls and the old Alcántara Bridge. They also put in a drainage system which, in some parts, remained in use until well into the 20th century.

Due to the crisis in the Roman Empire, the city fell easily to the attack of the Alani in 411 and was taken shortly afterwards in 418 by the Visigoths. Later, in 554, Athanagild established his court in Toledo, which became the official capital of the Visigothic monarchy and an archbishopric in 569 under Leovigild. Thus began a period of splendour, reflected in the famous Councils of Toledo. These were general assemblies of a political and religious nature that were convoked by the king and presided over by the archbishop of Toledo. The councils drew up religious dogma and also dealt with legal and political issues. The third council, held in 589 and called together by King Recared and presided over by Saint Leander, was particularly important. Here, the King rejected Arianism and converted to Catholicism, laying the foundations for the political and religious unification of Spain. At the eighth council, held in 653 and convoked by Recceswinth, the most important code of law of the period, the *Liber Iudiciorum*, was promulgated. In the same period in 674, King Wamba strengthened the city walls, which went as far as the Sun Gate to the north. The Visigothic cathedral was on the same site as the current building and Toledo at that time shone with the splendour and majesty of its palaces and

Museum of the Councils and of Visigothic Culture: fragments of the Credo from the mass sculpted in stone (7th century) found next to the Shrine of the Cristo de la Vega.

churches. However, no complete building has survived to allow us to appreciate this legacy. Of the limited remains, some were used for later buildings, while others have been put into the collection now housed in the Museum of the Councils and Visigothic Culture in the Church of San Román.

The arrival of the Muslims in Toledo in 711, the same year in which they entered the peninsula, saw the beginning of a new phase in the city. This profoundly marked the city and is characterised, in general terms, by an enriching cultural interchange brought about by the policy of religious tolerance. The population in Toledo came from diverse ethnic groups, consisting of Muslims (including renegades, former Christians who converted to Islam), Mozarabs (Christians who adopted Arab language and culture) and Jews (whose presence in Toledo dates back a long way). This population often rose up against the centralism of Cordoba. These uprisings were cruelly quashed, particularly on the so-called «Day of the Graveyard» in 807, also known as the «Night of Toledo», when all the members of the aristocracy were beheaded. The city was restored to a degree of peace under the rule of Abd ar-Rahman III, when it became a particularly important cultural centre. When the Caliphate of Cordoba fell in 1035, Toledo became a major city of the Moorish kingdom and remained so until the spring of 1085, when it was conquered by the Christian troops of Alfonso VI, the king of Castile and León.

During the almost 400 years of Muslim domination, the city, then known as Tulaitula, had taken on the urban shape that has come down to us today, with its characteristic labyrinth of narrow streets. The city also grew northwards through the creation of the Santiago and Antequeruela suburbs. Already at that time a clearly established city, there was no substantial change to its shape following the Christian conquest of 1085, due in part to the fact that its surrender had been agreed by a pact, leading to no urban destruction, and also in part to the admiration aroused by Islamic art. From that time onwards, because of the limited land available within

The old centre is a sea of roofs all crammed in together in the maze of narrow streets.

the walls, Toledo has always rebuilt itself upon its old foundations.

As already mentioned, the co-existence of Muslims, Jews and Christians lasted until the time Toledo passed into Christian hands in 1085. It was especially during this second phase of the «Toledo of the Three Cultures» when the city underwent its greatest cultural growth, arising from this tolerance, which was maintained, despite the occasional conflict. There can be no doubt that one of the best fruits of this period is the School of Translators of Toledo, whose work went on to influence western culture. While no school as such actually existed, the term refers to the group of translators who, in the 12th and 13th centuries, translated Arab texts and works by classical writers, such as Aristotle, Galen and Ptolemy, which

had been lost to the western world and existed only in an Arabic version. This work of outstanding importance was made possible by the presence in Toledo of Mozarabs and Jews who had mastered Arabic and Latin, and was heavily supported by leading figures of the time, including King Alfonso X the Wise. Added to this cultural splendour was economic growth and the growing power of the Church. Shortly after the Christian conquest, Pope Urban II made Toledo the leading city in the Spanish Catholic Church. The cathedral was established in the Great Mosque, which itself had been built on the site of the Visigothic cathedral. It was not until 1226 that building began on the Cathedral that stands today.

However, the imperial city of Toledo lost its political pre-eminence in 1561, when Philip II decided to move the capital of the kingdom to Madrid, which had a dramatic effect on the economy of the city. The 10,000 families to be found at the end of the 16th century fell in number to only 5,000 in 1646. It was only the power of the Church that prevented a greater decline as Toledo remained the spiritual capital of Spain. The archbishops of Toledo always played an important role as the patrons of culture and as the driving forces behind major building projects.

In the 18th century, the city blossomed through the presence of a prosperous textile industry when the Real Compañía de Comercio y Fábricas was set up in 1748, but this economic resurgence was only a temporary respite. Toledo was also important during a number of historic events, such as the War of Independence, during which the Alcázar was set on fire by French troops (1810), and the Civil War, when the Alcázar was the setting of a famous siege (1936). The major revitalisation of the city came about in 1983, when it was made the capital of the autonomous community of Castile-La Mancha. Toledo had already experienced a new drive of industrialisation when it began to relieve congestion in Madrid. Despite all this, the city itself remains its greatest legacy. It is undoubtedly one of the most interesting cities in the world.

The coat of arms on the Gate of San Martín carries the columbines and imperial arms of the city of Toledo.

New Bisagra Gate.

A BASTION ON THE TAGUS: the castles, walls, gates and bridges of Toledo.

Encircled by river and wall
It vaunts its heroic majesty

As these lines by Lope de Vega reveal, the city at first sight appears to be an impregnable bastion. You need to draw closer to its gates and to reach the banks of the river to discover the bridges, which offer the first welcome to the hospitality of Toledo. The city is surrounded to the east, south and west by the curving sweep of the Tagus, while to the north it is linked to the undulating plain of the plateau of Castile. The main, though not the oldest, gateway, the **New Bisagra Gate**, opens up on this side. This gate was originally built under the Muslims but was completely reconstructed in 1550 during the reign

of Charles V by Alonso de Covarrubias. The exterior façade has two large semicircular fortified towers and an enormous city coat of arms, which make it a very elegant building. Beyond the arch, there is a parade ground and a second section, with a façade inside the walls, that culminates in two towers crowned with tiled capitals. Barely 80 metres separate this entrance from the **Old Bisagra Gate**, also known as the Alfonso VI Gate in order to distinguish it from the other gateway and because it is said that the king's troops entered the city through it when they conquered Toledo in the spring of 1085. The name of both these gateways derives from the Arabic word *Bab-Shagra*, or Gate of La Sagra, because it opens out onto the broad plain to the north and the district known as La Sagra. This older gate retains a large part of its original structure, which dates from the 11th century. Protected by two strong fortified towers,

The Old Bisagra or Alfonso VI Gate: interior and exterior façades.

Interior façade of the Valmardón Gate.

The Sun Gate, built in the 14th century like a flanking tower, connected the precincts of the Rabad or suburb with the medina.

its outer façade has three arches, the central one being circular and the side arches being pointed. Under the great central arch, there is a new hewn horseshoe arch with lintel through which you pass into the city. Opposite the Old Bisagra Gate, in what is now Avenida de la Caba, there is the *maqbara*, or Muslim cemetery, demonstrating the importance of this gate in its time. Passing inwards, you enter the suburb of Santiago.

Further on into the city at the end of Calle Real del Arrabal, where the Visigothic walls to the north used to end, there is the **Gate of Bab-al-Mardum** or **Valmardón Gate**. This gate dates back to the 10th century and is the oldest one in existence, although it has undergone some changes over the course of its history. The original horseshoe arch, for example, was altered to turn it into a half point arch.

The **Sun Gate** very nearby was built in the 14th century in the Mudejar style, undoubtedly to make it easier to reach the centre in comparison with the steep slope that coaches needed to climb to cross through the Valmardón Gate. As it is embedded into the wall, this gateway serves as both a flanking tower and as a military gate. The medallion that decorates it was added in the 16th century and represents the Imposition of the Chasuble of Saint Ildefonso under the moon and the sun, which is where the name the gate is known by today comes from. In the upper part, between the interlaced arches, there is a small window and a relief portraying St. Peter's denial of his Lord, which comes from a 4th-century Paleochristian sarcophagus.

Following along walls, the next gate is the **Gate of los Alarcones**, which has a similar structure. It underwent considerable change in the 17th century, when a conventual building was incorporated into it. The next stretch of wall was demolished in order to allow the city

Detail of the Sun Gate showing the medallion which portrays the descent of Our Lady to impose the chasuble on St. Ildefonso, archbishop of Toledo, which according to tradition occurred in 666 in thanks for the defence that the saint had made of his chastity.

The
Alcántara
Gate.

Detail of the fortified tower of the Alcántara Bridge.

Detail of the arch of the Alcántara Bridge.

to expand. In general, however, there still remains a large part of the **walls** that defended Toledo, starting from the Visigothic period and then later reinforced and extended by the Muslims, and then strengthened again after the Christian reconquest. The best section of wall, with several circular fortified towers, is to be found between the Old Bisagra Gate and Cambrón Gate.

After the Gate of los Alarcones comes the **Alcántara Gate**. This gate is Arab in origin, as demonstrated by its angle. It faces the **Alcántara Bridge** and was the main entrance to the *al-Hizam*, the military area with the citadel and palace of the governors during the Muslim period and the north-westerly district which occupied the most prominent site in the city (where the Alcázar is now located). Its name comes from the Arabic word *Al-Qantara*, which means bridge, even though the bridge was in fact first put up during the Roman era. The bridge

was later reconstructed at the end of the 10th century due to its poor condition and then again in 1258 when King Alfonso X ordered that it be rebuilt following serious damage caused by a flood. The west fortified tower dates from this last reconstruction, although it was later adapted under the rule of the Catholic Monarchs, whose coat of arms decorate its walls. The east tower was replaced in 1721 by a Baroque arch to make it easier for carts to enter the city.

Between this bridge and the New Alcántara Bridge is the **Artificio Juanelo** –Juanelo Device– which is a famous scheme invented by the engineer Juanelo Turriano to draw water from the Tagus up to the Alcázar and which remained in use up to the 19th century. Just beyond the New Alcántara Bridge on both banks of the river are the ruins of the **Roman aqueduct**, which it is estimated rose to a height of over 70 metres.

The Alcántara Bridge and city with the Alcázar.

Near the Alcántara Bridge is the **Castle of San Servando**, which dominates a hill. This strategic location between the city and the broad plain irrigated by the Tagus, called the King's Orchard, meant that the castle always controlled this entrance to Toledo. Apparently of Visigothic origins, it was adapted by the Arabs and later restored following the Christian conquest to house a Cluniac monastery (hence the origin of its name). The castle subsequently passed into the hands of the order of the Templars. Archbishop Tenorio ordered that it be rebuilt in the 14th century as it was practically destroyed. It then fell into disuse and has once again been recently restored, this time as a youth hostel.

Further away, in the King's Orchard, is the **Galiana Palace**, with its lofty crenellated towers. The current, privately-owned, building was reconstructed in the 14th century and replaces a former castle that was re-nowned for its lovely gardens and sumptuous drawing rooms and because the beautiful Galiana, daughter of the Moorish king Galafre who became Charlemagne's wife, lived here.

There is another entrance to the ancient walled city at the same level as the New Alcántara Bridge. This is the **Gate of the Twelve Songs**, which has a horseshoe arch. The **Iron Gate**, located next to the House of the Diamond Merchant, is also of Muslim origin. All that remains now of this gate is an impressive fortified tower. The final gate that has been conserved down to the present day is the **Cambrón Gate** in the west of the city. This was completely rebuilt in the 16th century and consists of two floors which were fitted out as the governor's home. The façade inside the walls bears the coat of arms of Philip II and an image of St. Leocadia, the patron saint of Toledo, which is attributed to Berruguete.

The Galiana Palace in the King's Orchard.

The Castle of San Servando.

The Cambrón Gate, interior and exterior façades.

Outside it carries the city's coat of arms. The name of the gate comes from the thorn that took root in one of its towers.

Below the Cambrón Gate there is the second bridge, the **San Martín Bridge**, that has served as a crossing over the Tagus River since times long gone by. Originally there was a pontoon bridge, of which only one of the abutments now remains: this is a tower popularly known as the **Bath of La Cava** after the legend about the love between Florinda de la Cava, the daughter of Count Julian, and Don Rodrigo. This early bridge was destroyed by a heavy flood, leading to the construction of the San Martín Bridge. However, during the second half of the 14th century, as a result of the fighting between Peter I and his brother Henry of Trastámara, the bridge was badly damaged and had to be rebuilt. Tradition has it that the master builder responsible for this ambitious project realised that he had miscalculated the measurements of the central arch and that when the temporary framework to support the construction was removed everything would collapse. In despair at not being able to find any way of righting the problem, he told his wife of his worries. One night, she secretly set fire to the work. The fire was believed to be an accident and the master builder was able to construct the bridge again, this time using the correct calculations and without any damage to his reputation. According to the legend, this determined woman is the figure that decorates the keystone of the central arch, although in reality it is a portrayal of Archbishop Tenorio, who had the bridge built. The bridge still has its two defensive towers: the outer one dates from the 13th century and the inner one, with the city's coat of arms flanked by two representations of the emperor, dates from the 16th century.

San Martín Bridge and the eastern tower. In the background high up is the Monastery of San Juan de los Reyes.

San Martín Bridge and Bath of La Cava.

Night shot of the Cathedral.

THE CATHEDRAL

Built on the same site as the principal church of the reign of Recared and as the Great Mosque, the building now standing was begun in 1226 on the orders of Archbishop Jiménez de Rada during the reign of Ferdinand III, also known as Saint Ferdinand. The main part of the church was completed in 1493. The large church (140 metres long and 130 metres wide) is built on a Latin cross with a main nave and four central aisles which end in a double ambulatory and a transept without a dome. It is roofed with ogival arches that are widely splayed to make space for large stained glass windows. The lines of the church are attributed to the maestros Martín and Petrus Petri, although many artists contributed to the extraordinary work, the *dives toledana*, which is considered as a whole to be the earliest and most impressive of the cathedrals built in Spain during the Gothic period. Seen from the outside from the limited space left to it by the city's growth, the Cathedral perhaps lacks the awe-inspiring presence of other great Spanish and European Gothic churches. Nevertheless, the decorative wealth of its doors and especially the extensive collection of treasures kept in its interior are truly astonishing.

The main façade, which was begun in 1418, has three porches which are named according to the allegorical representations that decorate them: the central one is the Door of Forgiveness, with a sculptural group that portrays the Last Supper; to the right is the Scribes Door, known as the Door of Judgement; and to the left is the Tower Door, known as the Door of Hell. The building has a single tower, which is finished off with a flamboyant slender spire. The central group of bells holds the Fat Bell, so-called because of its extraordi-

View of the main façade of the Cathedral, the main church of Toledo, which looks out onto Plaza del Ayuntamiento.

The Lion Gate.

nary size and weight. The bell, cast in 1753, is 10 metres in circumference, 12 metres high and weighs 17,744 kilos.

In Calle Arco del Palacio, The Mollete Door, also known as the Door of Justice, leads into the cloister. *Mollete* means bread roll and here soft bread was distributed to the poor. The Clock Door is set in the north side. Lastly, the Lion Door, the magnificent work by Enrique Egas in Flamboyant Gothic, and the Plain Door, the simplest in the building are set in the south side. Inside the Cathedral, the choirstalls finely worked by Rodrigo Alemán, Felipe Vigarny and Alonso de Berruguete are particularly worthy of attention. There is also the Sanctuary protected by a beautiful grille done by Villalpando and presided over by an immense altarpiece in Flamboyant Gothic style. There is the famous *Transparente,* the Baroque work by Narciso

Tomé. The Chapter House, with its splendid coffered ceiling and frescos by Juan de Borgoña, holds portraits of all the archbishops of Toledo. The Sacristy houses the Cathedral Museum: below a vault painted by Luca Giordano, there is an exhibition of paintings by El Greco (including *The Disrobing of Christ*), Goya, Van Dyck, Tristán and other artists. The Cathedral Treasure, in the Chapel of San Juan, includes a superb processional custodial, an outstanding piece of Spanish goldwork, and the Bible of St. Louis, which dates from the 13th century. Other important chapels are those of San Ildefonso, which occupies the central section of the ambulatory and which has magnificent sepulchres; and the Corpus Christi, or Mozarabic, Chapel designed by Enrique Egas and erected on the orders of Cardinal Cisneros in 1500 to celebrate mass once again according to the old Mozarabic ritual.

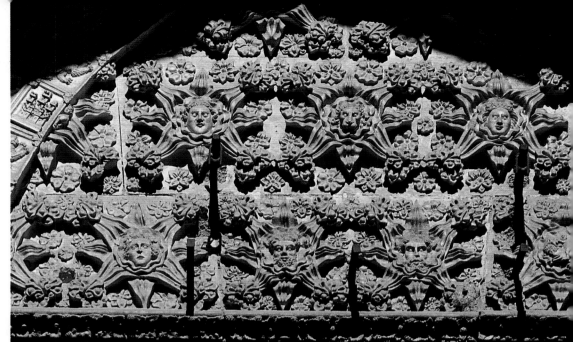

Detail of the sculptures that decorate the Gate of Hell.

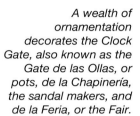

A wealth of ornamentation decorates the Clock Gate, also known as the Gate de las Ollas, or pots, de la Chapinería, the sandal makers, and de la Feria, or the Fair.

Our Lady of the Tabernacle, *in the shrine of the same name, is the patron saint of the city and the image most worshipped by the people of Toledo. This lovely carving, which tradition has it stood on the high altar of the original Visigothic Church of Santa María de Toledo, dates from the 13th century and is made of wood covered in silver.*

The cloister, decorated with frescoes painted by Bayeu and Maella between 1776 and 1782, is Gothic in style. It is built on the same site as the alcaná, or Jewish market.

The Transparente *by Narciso Tomé (1721-1732) was the last major architectural work carried out on the Cathedral. In order to provide more lighting in the niche where the Holy Sacrament is kept behind the main chapel, the artist was commissioned to undertake this work, which even today arouses as much praise as it does criticism for its damage to the Gothic harmony of the church. In order to create the work, a large opening was cut into the vaulting, enabling the sun to shine brightly into the semi-darkness. A large number of marble figures with various bronze details make up this large altarpiece that rises up to the opening itself in the vault.*

The harmony of the aisles and the fine smooth surface of the timbers mix with the detailing of the grilles and the painstaking decoration of a wall.

The stained glass windows, together with the Transparente are the keys to the secret of the light and shade that seem to make up the Cathedral of Toledo.

The choirstalls are one of the most important examples of the Castilian Renaissance. The lower part was carved by Rodrigo Alemán, while the upper part was carved by Felipe Vigarny and Alonso de Berruguete.

The Chapterhouse is the masterpiece by Juan de Borgoña, who painted the frescoes on the walls. The frieze that runs around the room shows the portraits of the archbishops of Toledo, starting at the top with St. Eugene to Cisnernos, also painted by Juan de Borgoña, while below are those that come after Cisneros and painted by a number of different artists. These are all half-length portraits and below each one is the name of the archbishop and the date. The magnificent coffered ceiling was done by Diego López Arenas and Francisco de Lara between 1504 and 1508.

The processional monstrance made by Enrique de Arfe between 1517 and 1524 is the jewel in the Cathedral treasure and was undoubtedly the first of its kind. The monstrance is made of solid silver, gold and precious gems, and consists of 5,600 pieces.

In the Cathedral Sacristy there is the magnificent portrait of Pope Paul III by Titian. The Cathedral Museum has an impressive collection of paintings, tapestries and goldwork, as well as a large number of dalmatics, chasubles and embroidered mitres, which are all held in the Sacristy and in the buildings of the octagonal room or Reliquary, in the Vestry and in the New Rooms of the Cathedral Museum, which were set up in the former Treasury and Counting-house.

The Disrobing of Christ, *a masterpiece by El Greco, together with the* Burial of the Count of Orgaz, *presides over the high altar in the Sacristy. This large painting was commissioned from the artist by the Cathedral Chapter and painted between 1575 and 1577. It represents the Saviour stripped of His raiment before the crucifixion.*

The White Virgin, sculpted in alabaster, is a magnificent Gothic carving of French origin and dating back to the 14th century. This touching happy image of motherhood presides over the Prime Altar in the Cathedral Choir.

The Bible of St. Louis (13th century) consists of three codices profusely painted with miniatures which contain biblical texts and moral commentaries. The photograph shows a fragment of The Creation from the first folio.

Travellers of yesteryear used to talk of the beauty of the Cathedral on moonlit nights. Today, thanks to technology, we can look upon it illuminated by a light that may be less romantic but certainly shines more brightly.

Main façade of the Tránsito Synagogue.

Gate to the Jewish Quarter in Calle del Angel.

THE JEWISH QUARTER OF TOLEDO

It is not certain when the first Jews arrived in Toledo, but it is known that they were already an important community during Visigothic rule. In addition, the policy of religious tolerance practised after the Muslim conquest enabled a prosperous Jewish community to develop, which was to acquire great prestige at all levels between the 12th and 14th centuries. It is not surprising to note that Toledo was considered the Jerusalem of Spain. However, the various periods of persecution that Jews were subjected to by the Christian population led to a decline in the Jewish population. In 1492, the Catholic Monarchs finally decreed that Jews should be expelled. This resulted in the ultimate disappearance of the former Jewish quarter of Toledo, although the body of evidence of this community that still exists is one of the most important in Europe.

The two Jewish areas that then existed, the *Alcaná* and the *Madinat-al-Yahud*, took shape during the period of Muslim domination in the 9th century. The *Alcaná* was situated in what is now the Cathedral cloister and neighbouring streets. This was a neighbourhood of rich merchants who enjoyed great renown because of the rich variety and quality of their products, but the area was virtually destroyed in 1391 due to the general persecution of Jews throughout the peninsula by both Christians and Muslims alike, who were motivated by a thirst for revenge and by envy of certain Jewish tax collectors or those who had grown rich through usury. When the Cathedral cloister was built, this Jewish quarter disappeared for good.

The *Madinyat-al-Yahud*, or Greater Neighbourhood,

was separated from the city by an inner wall and took up a large part of the south-eastern area of the old centre. Its main artery was Calle del Angel, where there is still the **Gate to the Jewish Quarter**, a horseshoe arch set into the wall that protected the neighbourhood. Only two of the various synagogues still exist and they show signs of later adaptations. The **Santa María la Blanca Synagogue** appears to have been the main synagogue. It was built in the 12th century in the Mudejar style with influences from Almohad art. It has an irregular floor plan and five aisles separated by horseshoe arches on octagonal capitals. In 1405, following the preachings of St. Vicente Ferrer in Toledo, a great crowd went to the Jewish quarter to occupy the synagogue, which was converted into a church dedicated to Saint Mary. Three chapels were later added at the top and it still served as a barracks and storehouse as late as the 18th century. Nowadays it is run by a community of cloistered nuns.

Nearby is the **El Tránsito Synagogue**, also known by the name of its founder Samuel Levi, who was the royal treasurer to Peter I of Castile. This synagogue was built in 1356 and handed over to the Knights of Calatrava after the expulsion of the Jews. The interior is extremely beautiful: the walls are decorated with fine plasterwork and there is a magnificent panelled ceiling in the Mudejar style. The Sephardic Museum is sited here and shows the full history of the Jews in Spain.

Santa María la Blanca Synagogue.

General view of San Juan de los Reyes from the Cambrón Gate.

SAN JUAN DE LOS REYES

Near the Cambrón Gate, set right in the heart of the Jewish quarter, is the Monastery of San Juan de los Reyes, founded by the Catholic Monarchs to commemorate their victory in the battle at Toro on 1 March 1476 over the forces of Alfonso V of Portugal and the Castilian aristocracy who were fighting for Juana la Beltraneja to succeed to the throne of Castile. The building was also planned as the royal pantheon, although the conquest of the Kingdom of Granada led to a change in this initial proposal. The monastery was then given into the care of Franciscan monks, who remain in what is now the Franciscan Monastery de la Concepción. The monastery suffered considerable losses due to the War of Independence. The French set fire to it, as they did to the Alcázar and other buildings, before leaving Toledo. Its decline was exacerbated by the confiscation of church goods in 1836, involving the expulsion of the monastery's inhabitants. Restoration later began and Franciscans returned to occupy it in 1954.

Designed to appear aristocratic and triumphant (the decoration inside is especially replete with heraldic motifs), San Juan de los Reyes is a masterpiece of the Flamboyant Gothic, although like everything in Toledo it still has Mudejar influences. The designer was Juan Guas, the Breton architect and sculptor who also worked on the Cathedral and who was responsible for the magnificent palace of the Duke of Infantado in Guadalajara. Juan Guas started the works in 1477 and remained in control until his death in 1496. The brothers Enrique and Antón Egas were his principal collaborators on the project, and they continued until work finished in 1506, when the cloister was completed. From the outside, the central section of the church looks similar to a tumulus and pinnacles, or to wax candles at a vigil. Originally, the main door opened at the foot of the church but in the 16th century this was blocked up and the side door was redesigned and became the principal entrance. At the top, the building is finished off by an impressive octagonal dome. This part of the church is where most of the external decoration is to be found: statues, heraldic devices, blind arcades, etc. The chains hanging from the walls are those of the Christian prisoners freed after the taking of the Kingdom of Granada.

Inside, the there is a splendid cupola and lavish decoration, particularly in the area of the presbytery, which was originally expected to serve as the royal pantheons. The original altarpiece was destroyed during the War of Independence and was replaced by the one we see today which is the work of Francisco Comontes and comes from the Hospital de la Santa Cruz. The two-storey richly decorated cloister is also worthy of note. Access to the upper floor is via a beautiful staircase designed by Covarrubias.

Main façade of the Church of San Juan de los Reyes.

The high cloister is covered with a wooden coffered ceiling inscribed with the emblems of the kingdoms of the Catholic Monarchs, as well as their arms (the yoke and arrows) and their initials.

The low cloister has a profusion of delicately sculpted decoration.

Partial view of the cloister, with its mixed linear arcades in the upper part and fine Flamboyant tracery in the lower part.

San Juan de los Reyes has a dazzling wealth of beautiful decorative ornamentation. The illustrations show a detail of the presbytery wall and two details of the cloister.

The Church of San Román: the central aisle and Chancel.

THE CHURCH OF SAN ROMÁN AND THE MUSEUM OF THE COUNCILS AND OF VISIGOTHIC CULTURE

One of the most noticeable towers of all those that stand out above the roofs of old Toledo is that of San Román, which, until the Cathedral was built, was the loftiest in the city, in addition to being built upon the highest part of the old centre. It was for this reason, according to tradition, that Alfonso VIII, still a boy at the time, was here proclaimed king of Castile in 1166. The latest section of the tower, however, dates from the end of the 13th or early 14th centuries. It was originally longer and connected to the church. It has a square layout and characteristic Mudejar decoration. The origins of the church itself are unknown, although it is one of the oldest in Toledo. It was certainly already in place during the Visigothic period, to which many of the capitals belong. It was then used as a mosque and rebuilt at the beginning of the 13th century in the Mudejar style. It is laid out like a basilica, with three aisles separated by three large horseshoe arches of the Caliphate type. The main chapel, however, is Plateresque and is the result of restoration work by Alonso de Covarrubias. The high altarpiece is by Diego de Velasco. The most interesting feature, nevertheless, is the murals, which are one of the few examples of Romanesque art in Toledo. They date from the 13th century and combine Christian elements with the geometric and plant motifs of Arabic decoration. Since 1969, the Church of San Román has housed the Museum of the Councils and of Visigothic Culture. The collection holds a number of important pieces from the period, including reproductions of the famous treasure of Guarrazar.

One to the main attractions in the Church of San Román are the frescos that decorate the walls and arches (13th century). In the picture, the scene shown represents the resurrection of the dead.

Mosque of Cristo de la Luz.

OTHER CHURCHES IN TOLEDO

We have already looked at the main religious buildings in Toledo: the Cathedral, the synagogues of Santa María la Blanca and El Tránsito, the Monastery of San Juan de los Reyes and the Church of San Román. But there are still many more churches in the city to admire. Undoubtedly one of the aspects about Toledo that most surprises visitors to the city is the number of churches and monasteries. It must not be forgotten that from the year 400, Toledo was the setting of the most important Church councils and that following the Christian conquest, it became the ecclesiastical capital of Spanish Catholicism. While some no longer exist or have been put to other uses, it is important to note that until the laws suppressing religious orders and confiscating their property were passed in the 19th century, there were some 40 monasteries and convents, truly an astonishing figure, in addition to the various parish churches, hospices and other charitable institutions. Many of these monasteries are enclosed orders, and so the church can only be visited during Mass. You can of course still go up to the doors, not solely to admire their evident artistry but also because these buildings represent an essential part of the soul of Toledo.

The former **Cristo de la Luz Mosque** dates back from before the Christian conquest. It is still virtually intact and constitutes the most important example of Islamic art in Toledo. According to the inscription in Cufic characters on the main façade, it was built in 999 by the architect Musa ibn Ali. The floor plan is almost a square and is structured by four columns with Visigothic capitals that form an area with three

Tower of the Church of El Salvador, which used to be a minaret in a former mosque.

aisles crossed by another three, thereby creating nine different spaces, each of which is covered by a differently decorated vault, following the models of the *maqsura* in Cordoba. The Mudejar apse and presbytery were added to the building in the 13th century.

Legend has it that there was already a sanctuary here during Visigothic times. However, when Muslim troops were just about to arrive in 711 and to prevent its profanation, the image of Christ that was venerated was hidden in a hollow in a wall and left there with a burning oil lamp. When Alfonso VI entered Toledo in victory in 1085, the royal train stopped in front of the mosque and the king's horse knelt down, making it impossible to continue. Everyone was surprised by this and took it as a sign from God. The king's men then set about searching the small building until they came across the hidden image of Christ and the lamp that was still burning. Marvelling at this astonishing find, an altar was immediately improvised, with the king's own shield serving as a cross, and the first mass was held. The mosque was consecrated as a shrine and named Cristo de la Luz (Christ of the Light). To commemorate the event, a white paving slab was placed facing the entrance in the spot where the king's horse knelt.

The **Mosque de Tornerías** is a further Muslim religious building that still exists. It is to be found in the street of the same name and its first floor now houses the Centre for Promoting the Arts and Crafts of Castile-La Mancha. This was undoubtedly a private oratory, which would explain its unusual location on the upper floor. It dates from the 11th century and is laid out in a similar manner to the Cristo de la Luz Mosque.

Various decorative elements in the **Church of El Salvador** make it clear that this church was also used as a mosque. Visigothic columns and capitals were used in its construction and there is also an interesting Visigothic pilaster with anthropomorphic carv-

Church of San Sebastián.

Church of San Lucas. In the background up on the mountain, there is the Conde de Orgaz National Parador hotel.

ings, that were disfigured due to the Muslim rules forbidding the representation of human figures.

The **Belén Chapel** is another piece of important evidence of the Muslim period. This small 11th century chapel in the Caliphate style has an octangular interior. It is located inside the precincts of the **Santa Fe Monastery,** which is now used as the Provincial Library and Archive, and which was built upon the former residence of the emirs –the famous Galiana Palaces–, because of this it is thought that the chapel was a private oratory in the sumptuous home. The sepulchre of Fernán Pérez, son of Ferdinand III the Saint and who died in 1242, is housed here. In addition to the Mudejar sepulchre, there are interesting frescoes on the walls which were done during the reign of the Catholic Monarchs.

During the period of Muslim rule, the Christian population (the Mozarabs) were permitted to keep their churches open and to continue practising the old Visigothic liturgy, also known as the Mozarabic and Toledan liturgy because Toledo was the most important centre for this community, which still exists today. Attempts were made to impose the liturgy of the Church of Rome after the Christian conquest, leading to a number of conflicts. Eventually, an agreement was reached whereby the privileges of the Mozarabs were guaranteed. This meant that all their parish churches could be maintained, and over the course of time they have all been rebuilt. There were a total of six Mozarabic churches dotted around the city which survived after the conquest, some of which still have signs of their Visigothic origins. This is the case with the churches of **Santa Eulalia, of San Sebastián, of San Lucas** and of **Santa Justa y Rufina.** The Visigothic ritual was almost completely abandoned in 1500, when Cardinal Cisneros ordered the building of the Corpus Christi Chapel or Mozarabic Chapel in order to ensure that it was not lost. In order to restore it in full, he had all the codices and manuscripts that existed gathered together and even drew up the missal and breviary again.

When you approach these churches, it is evident that some of them still today have the outlines of the Mudejar style, which so characterises the city. Mudejar art is a typically Hispanic product and very representative of Toledo because it is the fruit of certain specific historic circumstances: the survival of Muslim culture under Christian rule. It is, in short, a style where we see the merging of elements of both cultures, particularly the eastern tradition, to which the Jewish synagogues were also closely related. Characteristic features of every Mudejar work are the use of bricks and rough stone as the main building materials with decoration based on the use of a profusion of plasterwork, multicoloured tiles and worked wooden roofing.

Most of the churches in Toledo are Mudejar, although they have all had later additions. The **Church of San Andrés** is an especially interesting place to visit because elements from all periods can be found here.

Church of San Andrés.

Church of Santiago del Arrabal.

There is also the **Convent of Santa Isabel la Real** founded in 1477 by María Suárez de Toledo and endowed by her with various family palaces, including Mudejar buildings; a complex to which the ancient parish church of San Antolín, with its beautiful Mudejar apse, was added. The **Church of San Bartolomé** has a high tower and great variety of arches in the apses. The tower of the **Church of Santo Tomé** is a fine example of its type. The church which has preserved most of its Mudejar characteristics is that of **Santiago del Arrabal,** which was built in the 13th century. The tower dates further back to the 12th century and might even be the minaret of an ancient mosque given its shape and the distribution of the staircases. The church has three aisles closed at the top with three semicircular apses that are decorated on the outside, as are the doors, with a large variety of small blind

arches. Of note inside are the wooden coffered ceilings and the Mudejar plasterwork pulpit. The Plateresque high altarpiece is by Francisco de Espinosa.

The **Church of Cristo de la Vega** outside the walls at the end of the Paseo del Circo Romano is another important Mudejar work. It formed part of the former Visigothic Basilica of Santa Leocadia, where various Councils of Toledo were held. Only the apse and presbytery remain from its original building, that dates back to the end of the 13th century. The shrine is especially popular because to the image of Christ of the Vega, whose unnailed arm has given rise to many legends, including the famous poem by José Zorrilla *To a Good Judge, a Better Witness,* which recounts the story of the love of Diego Martínez and Inés de Vargas. One day, the young man from Toledo is called

ECCLESIÆ ✝ ALTARE ✝ IPSE ✝ CHRISTVS

Santiago del Arrabal: the high altar.

Mudejar apse in the Church of San Vicente.

High altar in the Shrine of Cristo de la Vega, presided over by the popular image of the Crucified Christ with unnailed arm.

Mudejar Convent of Santa Isabel la Real.

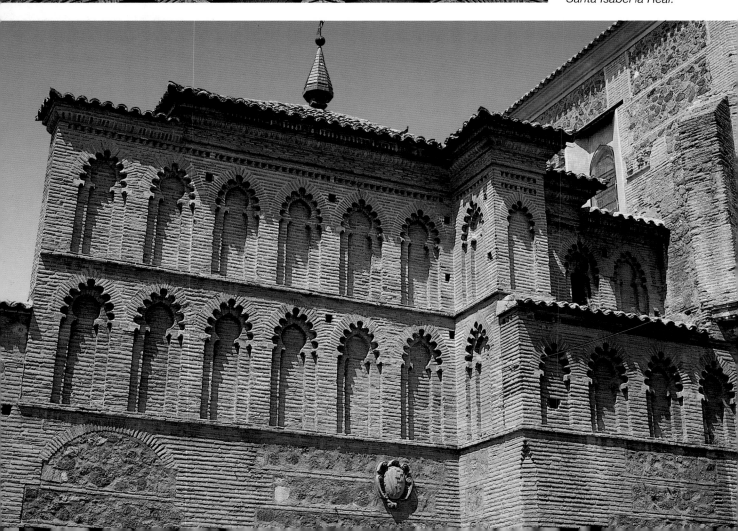

Façade of San Clemente, a magnificent sculptural work by Alonso de Covarrubias.

A large canvas by Francisco Rizi hangs over the high altar in the Convent of the Agustinas Calzadas.

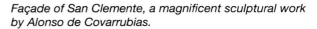

up to join the war. Before he leaves, he takes Inés to the to the shrine and swears before the image of Christ that he loves her and that he will marry her upon his return. After many years fighting, Diego Martínez returns to Toledo but, to Inés' surprise, denies that he had promised to wed her. Inés calls for justice and turns to the courts, with the Christ de la Vega as her only witness. Everyone goes to the church and one of the judges asks the image to swear on the Bible and say if Inés is telling the truth. In response, Christ unnails his right arm while His voice echoes around the church, saying «I am a witness».

While there are a great number of Mudejar religious buildings, there are very few churches in Toledo that represent any other architectural style. Nevertheless, the Mudejar churches themselves have many later additions in other styles, as previously noted. The Cathedral and the Monastery of San Juan de los Reyes are examples of the Gothic style. The **Monastery of Santo Domingo el Antiguo,** designed by Juan Herrera, is Renaissance in style and is particularly interesting because of its connection with El Greco and the artistic works held in its own museum. There is also a magnificent Renaissance door to the **Monastery of San Clemente,** done by Alonso de Covarrubias. Examples of the Baroque are to be found in the **Church of San Ildefonso,** or St. John the Baptist; the **Monastery of San Pedro Mártir,** which is now used as council buildings; the church of the **Convent of the Agustinas Calzadas,** or of the Gaitanas as it is popularly known, where there is a large painting of the Virgin by Francisco Rizi; and the **Monastery of Santo Domingo el Real,** which was founded in the 14th century, although the church was rebuilt in the 17th century, with its beautiful door framed by a porch.

Façade of the Conventual Church of Santo Domingo el Real.

Tower of the Church of Santo Tomé, which houses the masterpiece by El Greco The Burial of the Count of Orgaz.

EL GRECO AND TOLEDO

El Greco and his work are both closely linked to Toledo, not just because he spent a large part of his life and developed his individual style of painting here, but also because, as Marañón states, «his great painting is the worry that oozes from the soul of the city.» Doménikos Theotokópoulos, who was named the El Greco (the Greek), was born in 1541 in Crete, which was then a protectorate of Venice. He soon moved to Venice and then later to Rome. He worked with the great Italian masters of the period in both of these cities.

Like other Italian artists, he was undoubtedly drawn by the works at El Escorial, and arrived in Spain between 1575 and 1576. He ended up in Toledo, where he received his first commission through the help of friends. This work was the high altarpiece for the conventual church of Santo Domingo el Antiguo, of which only two of the original canvases, the *Saints John* and *The Resurrection,* still remain in situ. Following this first commission, he did *The Disrobing of Christ* (1577-79) for the Cathedral and *The Martyrdom of St. Maurice* (1580-82) for El Escorial. However, Philip II did not like El Greco's individual style and the artist's connection with the court came to an end. In contrast, he was held in very high regard in Toledo, where he was in great demand amongst various churches and important patrons, which continued until his death until 1614.

Shortly after arriving from Italy, El Greco settled in Toledo and soon married Jerónima de las Cuevas, with whom he had one son, Jorge Manuel, who was born in 1578. It is known that he lived close to where the **Home and Museum of El Greco** is to be found. This building was constructed early in the 20th century by the Marquis of Vega-Inclán, using earlier construction work and recreating it with genuine furniture and household items from the 16th century, for the purpose of bringing together the scattered work by the artist. The museum opened in 1912 and now holds a considerable collec-

Courtyard in the Home and Museum of El Greco. Although El Greco was not born in Spain, he came to identify with the spirit of Toledo to the extent that he created his best work here in this city.

El Greco painted his personal vision of the city in View and Plan of Toledo *(1610-1614, Home and Museum of El Greco).*

The Burial of the Count of Orgaz *(1586-1588, Church of Santo Tomé).*

tion of work that dates mainly from the later part of the artists life, from 1600 to 1614. The works included the *View and Plan of Toledo* and an *Apostolado* (a work from the two series entitled Apostolado, representing the apostles and Christ). There is also the famous painting *The Repentant Peter,* which is an earlier work, dating from around 1585.

Other works that can be seen by El Greco in Toledo are in the **Museum of Santa Cruz,** which holds one of the artist's last and most impressive works, The *Assumption of the Virgin;* in the **Hospital de Tavera Museum,** which has *The Holy Family* and the statuette entitled *The Saviour,* one of the few carvings ever done by the artist; in the **Chapel of San José** (the private oratory for which El Greco painted three altarpieces, although the chapel now only holds a *Saint Joseph* and the *Coronation of the Virgin);* in the conventual church of **Santo Domingo el**

Antiguo, which has works that have already been mentioned and is where the artist is buried; in the Cathedral, which apart from *The Disrobing of Christ* also has another *Apostolado;* and in the **Church of Santo Tomé,** for which he painted *The Burial of the Count of Orgaz,* which is unquestionably one of his most famous works. Painted between 1586 and 1588, it portrays the miracle that took place in 1312 when, along the way to bury the Count, Saint Augustine and Saint Stephen appeared to lay the body in the tomb. One of the most interesting features in the painting is the gallery of people attending the burial, who are contemporaries of El Greco's, such as the gentleman who is looking directly at the viewer, and his son, the page who is carrying a torch and who has a handkerchief that bares the artist's signature in Greek. The upper part of the canvas represents the Gloria, which is where the soul of the dead man is being led.

General view and two details of the main façade of the former Hospital de la Santa Cruz.

HOSPITAL DE SANTA CRUZ MUSEUM

This is one of the most interesting museums in Toledo, both because of the wealth of its collection and because of the building that houses it. Built on the initiative of the great cardinal Pedro González de Mendoza, the Hospital de Santa Cruz was set up in 1494 to take in foundlings and served this purpose until 1846. Although the cardinal promoted the project, he did not even see work begun as he died in 1495. Nevertheless, he entrusted it to the executors of his will, Isabel the Catholic, for whom he served as confessor and advisor, and his successor as archbishop of Toledo, Cardinal Cisneros, who also promoted and acted as patron for various buildings around the city. In 1504, the first stone was eventually laid and the building was completed ten years later.

Enrique Egas, the queen's architect, was given responsibility for directing the works. Together with his brother Antón, he designed a large two-storey building on a Greek cross which was inspired by Filarete's plan for the Hospital of Milan. There were supposed to be four courtyards between the arms of the cross but only three were finished, one of which is very small in comparison with the whole construction. A number of famous artists worked with the Egas brothers, including Alonso de Covarrubias, who was responsible for the magnificent main door and the principal cloister. Covarrubias saw the door as the main façade of a great altarpiece. The tympanum has a representation of the *Invention of the Holy Cross by Saint Helena,* with the figure of Cardinal Mendoza worshipping the cross of Jerusalem, of which he was a pious devotee. Above is the *Embrace of St. Joachim and St. Anne before the Golden Gate* flanked by each patriarch. Both sculptural groups have a large number of figures and details, making this work one of the most superb examples of Spanish Plateresque style.

This detailing is also to be found in the interior in the doors to the vestibule, in the magnificent wooden panelled ceilings (with coffers on the vaults of the ground floor and with rafters and plugs for the upper

A view of the ground floor of the Santa Cruz Museum, with the chapel in the background.

floor), and in the pilasters of the transept, which finishes with a dome with Caliphate ribs. At the end of the north arm, where the entrance is, is the chapel covered by a beautiful ribbed vault.

The museum collection is divided into two sections: the Fine Arts and Archaeology. The Fine Arts are to be found on the first and second floor of the building, while Archaeology is housed in the main cloister and in an underground floor. The museum also has a representative sample of popular crafts from Toledo housed in the rooms underground.

There are many exceptional pieces worthy of mention in the Fine Arts section: the furnishings and weapons from the 16th century; various suits of armour; the busts of Charles V in repoussé silver and in marble, both of which date from the 16th century; a large collection of tapestries, including the 15th century Astrolabe tapestry; the standard that flew over the flag ship at the battle of Lepanto; the image of Christ which, according to legend, was found at the Mosque of Cristo de la Luz; ivory crucifixes; and many other items. More important still is the collection of paintings, with works by Ribera, Carducho, Morales, Giordano, Coello, Goya, a representative selection of 16th and 17th century painters from Toledo, and, of course, El Greco. The collection holds a total of some 20 paintings by El Greco from various churches throughout the city, although some of them are only attributed to him or copies. The painting which draws the greatest praise is undoubtedly *The Assumption of the Virgin,* one of El Greco's more daring works. This he painted in 1613, just one year before his death.

Bust of Charles V in repoussé silver (16th century).

The main cloister, as previously mentioned, is a magnificent work by Alonso de Covarrubias. The two-storey construction is almost square and has half pointed arches at ground floor level and segmental arches above. The coffered ceilings are also very attractive, as is the impressively sculpted staircase that links the two floors. It is here that the museum's archaeological collection is exhibited, with pieces from prehistory spanning right through to the period of Muslim rule.

View of the transept of the former Hospital de la Santa Cruz, revealing the delicate working of the pilasters.

A view of the main cloister of the former Hospital de la Santa Cruz.

One of the architects who has most left his mark on Toledo is Alonso de Covarrubias. In addition to the main façade for the Hospital de Santa Cruz, he also produced this marvellous staircase (1614).

The **Moor's Workshop** is a small but illustrative museum attached to the Santa Cruz Museum. It is given over to Mudejar art and crafts. It is to be found in the street of the same name and undoubtedly used to for part of Fuensalida Palace, with which it is linked though a courtyard. It has a main room and two side rooms, all of which are decorated with fine plasterwork and splendid wooden coffered ceilings. Its name comes from the fact that it used to be a workshop for the craftsmen working on the Cathedral, most of whom were Muslims or, more properly speaking Mudejars, great experts in the decorative arts. The same plasterwork that decorates these and the other rooms that can be seen are an excellent example of this art that is so characteristic of Toledo and that mixes Arab and Christian motifs, as we have already seen.

The austerity of the main façade of the Hospital de Tavera provides no suggestion of the wealth of treasures housed inside.

A view of the double courtyard designed by Alonso de Covarrubias for the Hospital de Tavera.

The Hospital de Tavera holds period furniture as well as important paintings.

THE HOSPITAL DE TAVERA AND THE DUKE DE LERMA FOUNDATION MUSEUM

The former Hospital de Tavera is one of the spots in Toledo where visitors feel most strongly that they are veritable guests of history. Here are the décor and furnishings so characteristic of the Castilian stately home of the 17th century. The pharmacy is still here, with its flasks, mortars, jars and other utensils as required in the 16th century. The archive is also conserved, with all its books and documents neatly arranged, just waiting to be consulted. It is known to the people of Toledo as the Hospital de Afuera (Outside) because it is beyond the walls. Its other local name is the Hospital of San Juan Bautista because it is dedicated to this John the Baptist. Its true name is

due to its founder, Cardinal Juan Tavera, who wanted to set up a great hospital, as had Cardinal Mendoza some decades before when he had the Hospital de Santa Cruz built. The Hospital de Tavera continued in use until the Spanish Civil War, when it was closed after suffering serious damage. The widowed Duchess of Lerma, the patron of the building and the house to which it belongs by virtue of continuing the charitable work begun by Cardinal Tavera, decided to restore it and to set up the Duke de Lerma Foundation Museum in the left wing by contributing period furniture and an impressive collection of paintings, in addition to the pharmacy and valuable hospital archive mentioned above.

Firstly, however, we must admire the building itself, which is one of the most interesting of the Spanish

A detail of the Holy Family painted towards 1595 by El Greco and now held in the Hospital de Tavera. For the delicate face of the Virgin, the artist took inspiration from that of his wife, who had already died some time before.

The Holy Family *by Tintoretto is another work in the artistic treasure kept in the Hospital de Tavera.*

Renaissance. It was built between 1542 and 1579, although the church dome was not completed until 1602 and the main façade has various later additions. The overall design is the work of Bartolomé Bustamante, who worked on the building until 1549, when Alonso de Covarrubias and the Vergaras took over. They created the beautiful unusual double courtyard around which the building itself is arranged. As we enter, to the left is the palace and museum; to the right are the buildings which now house the Historical Archives of the Nobility; facing us is the church.

One of the main attractions in the church is the magnificent sepulchre of Cardinal Tavera (1554), one of the last and most impressive works by Alonso de Berruguete, with its realism of heartrending simplicity. Also worthy of note is the high altarpiece, begun by El Greco although he died before completing it. His son Jorge Manuel finished the work. Of the various pieces by El Greco in the museum, there is a very interesting version of the *Holy Family,* in which it has been said the artist's own family is portrayed. There is also the *Portrait of Cardinal Tavera,* based on the death mask of the founder of the hospital; a version of the *Baptism of Christ;* and a small carving, *The Saviour,* which is one of the few sculptures ever done by El Greco. Other major paintings in the collection are José de Ribera's famous painting *The Bearded Woman;* Tintoretto's *Holy Family;* Zurbarán's *Portrait of the Duke de Medinaceli;* Sánchez Coello's *Portrait of Antonio Pérez,* secretary to Philip II; and Carreño's portraits of Queen Mariana of Austria and King John II of Portugal.

General view of the Alcázar, whose imposing outline rises up over the old centre of Toledo.

THE ALCÁZAR

Sited on the highest hill in the city, the Alcázar, or fortress, has always been a key element in Toledo's defensive system. It has almost been completely destroyed on several occasions during the course of its long history, although it has always risen again from its ashes. The strategic value of the site was noted by the Romans, who established a praetorium here. Later, during the time of the Visigoths, the royal abode of the Kingdom of Toledo was built nearby, although there are no remains of this palatial residence. Subsequently, under Muslim rule, a major fortification or *Al-Qasr* (the Arabic word from which Alcázar comes) was constructed as a royal residence and as a refuge for the garrison. The Alcázar

at that time was the setting for internal battles involving conflict between the authorities and the rebellious inhabitants of Toledo, which eventually led to political and economic autonomy from the centralism of the Caliphate of Cordoba. It is known that the Arab Alcázar of this time was destroyed and rebuilt on many occasions, with only the arch of a gateway to the lower section of the south-east fortified tower from the time of Al-Hakem (970) still remaining.

After Alfonso VI took the city, he ordered that the building be reconstructed in order to create a solid defence for the city of Toledo against possible Almohad attacks. According to tradition, El Cid the Champion was its first governor. The fortress was improved by the king's successors. Alfonso X the Wise, in particular, carried out extension work and is responsible for the east façade, which still has its crenellated battlements and circular fortified towers.

When the Muslim threat had disappeared in the 13th century due to the Christian victory at the Battle of Las Navas de Tolosa, the Alcázar was used as a residence by the royal family. One of the most oft-told stories of the Middle Ages is that of the imprisonment underground of Blanca de Bourbon on the orders of her husband Peter I the Cruel (1353). The room where the luckless wife was kept prisoner has been recreated in one of the underground rooms.

The Alcázar played a particularly important part during the Revolt of the Comuneros – a group of Castilian cities led by Toledo – in 1520-22. The main *comunero* leaders, such as Lasso de la Vega and Juan de Padilla, came from Toledo. The cities rebelled against the high taxes imposed by Emperor Charles I and in order to prevent future revolts, the Emperor, who made Toledo the capital of the empire, had the Alcázar rebuilt, which is when it acquired the imposing appearance that it has today.

Responsibility for the project was given to Alonso de Covarrubias, who worked with Villalpando, González de Lara and Juan de Herrera. The most noticeable features are the main door, which is the work of

Monument to Victory by Juan de Avalos next to the eastern façade of the Alcázar.

Main façade of the Alcázar done by Alonso de Covarrubias.

The Staircase of Honour, by Juan de Herrera according to designs by Covarrubias and Villalpando.

Covarrubias, presided over by an imperial shield flanked by the figures of the Visigothic monarchs Recared and Recceswinth; the large majestically elegant central courtyard; and the Staircase of Honour, with five flights of steps and covered by barrel vaulting, which was designed, like the courtyard, by Covarrubias and Villalpando.

When the court moved to Madrid in 1562, the Alcázar was used from time to time as accommodation for the royal family, and was then converted into a state prison in the middle of the 17th century. The first major fire in 1710, during the War of the Spanish Succession, destroyed a large part of the fort. It was then restored on the orders of Cardinal Lorenzana so that the Royal Almshouse could be established here. However, 100 years later in 1810 during the War of Independence, it was destroyed again by a second blaze when the French set fire to various buildings before leaving the city. A third fire, this time accidental, in 1887 burnt it down again. And once again the Alcázar was reconstructed and the Military Academy of Infantry was installed.

The building was reduced to rubble during the famous siege that occurred from 20 July to 28 September 1936 during the Civil War. Rebuilt yet again according to the design of Covarrubias, the Alcázar now houses the Museum of the Siege, with models and various items that recall this episode of the Civil War. The office of Colonel Moscardó, who led the defence of the Alcázar until the arrival of General Varela, is also preserved just as it was at the time.

Surrounded by elegant arcades, the courtyard of the Alcázar is presided over by a statue of the Emperor Charles I of Spain and V of Germany. This is a faithful reproduction of the statue sculpted by Leoni that is housed in Madrid in the Prado.

Plaza de Zocodover and the Arch of Blood.

THE STREETS AND SQUARES OF OLD TOLEDO

One of the defining features of the old city of Toledo is its nature as a monument. It is, in a manner of speaking, a veritable city-museum. It could be said that history has left no corner, no stone untouched. In this respect, there are few cities around the world as alive and as intact as Toledo. You can follow an itinerary taking you to the churches, main heritage sites or its museums. But if you really want to get to know the true spirit of Toledo, you need to get lost in the maze of its narrow streets. Strolling around Toledo like this, you will surely repeatedly come across the **Plaza de Zocodover,** the vital centre of the city since the Muslim period, more than once. Zocodover, with the hustle and bustle of its agora and the constant murmur going on underneath its arches, is the

central stage of Toledo. There is no better place for the visitor to observe all the comings and goings of the local population. The name comes from the Arabic *Suk-al-Dawab,* which means animal market. This wide esplanade originally separated the city from the *Al-Hizam,* the residence of the emirs, but ever since the very beginning there was always, until very recently, an open-air market here. The traditional weekly market has now moved to **Paseo del Carmen,** where it is held on a Tuesday. Other commercial areas stretch into the neighbouring streets, each of which used to specialise in a particular product. This trading continues today, as can be seen in **Calle Comercio** and **Calle Hombre de Palo.**

On the eastern side of the square that separated the *Al-Hizam* from the city is the **Arch of Blood.** The name refers to the Brotherhood of Blood, whose members

The Cathedral tower as seen from Calle de Santa Isabel.

Main façade of the Town Hall.

gave final consolation to those condemned to death, who were executed in the square. There also used to be the famous Blood Inn next to arch, where it is said that Miguel de Cervantes wrote *La Ilustre Fregona* (The Illustrious Kitchen Maid) and that was later destroyed during the Civil War.

Continuing along Calle Comercio and Calle Hombre de Palo, you come next to **Plaza del Ayuntamiento.** This square is dominated by the Cathedral, which faces the **Town Hall** and the Archbishop's Palace. Juan de Herrera was commissioned to build the Town Hall by the mayor Gómez Manrique, with work beginning in 1575. There is now barely any evidence of the original design as it was substantially altered by Jorge Manuel Theotokópoulos, the son of El Greco, at the beginning of the 17th century. Lastly, the two towers that finish in slate capitals were added by Teodoro de Ardemans.

The origins of the **Archbishop's Palace** date back to the 13th century, when King Alfonso VIII granted certain houses opposite the Cathedral to Archbishop Jiménez de Rada. Later, Cardinal Mendoza erected the arch that links the palace to the Cathedral. However, Cardinal Lorenzana ordered the destruction of almost the entire building and commissioned a new one from Ventura Rodríguez, who is responsible for a large part of the work but who died before it was completed. The façade that looks out onto the Cathedral dates from the time of Cardinal Tavera, whose coat of arms is shown. This part was built in 1545 and is the work of Covarrubias.

There is no doubt that one of the most attractive features of the city are the façades of the old palaces, and one of the most admired is the **Fuensalida Palace** in Paseo del Conde, next to the Church of

The Archbishop's Palace: the façade that faces out onto Plaza del Ayuntamiento.

Fuensalida Palace.

Baroque coat of arms of a former aristocrat's house in Calle de Rojas.

Santo Tomé. Built around 1440 by Pedro López de Ayala, the Lord of Fuensalida, and his wife Elvira Castañeda, whose coats of arms are shown on the façade, this large building is constructed around a magnificent courtyard that combines both the Gothic and Mudejar. In the courtyard, there is a bronze statue in memory of the Empress Isabel, wife of Charles V, who died here in this palace in 1539. It is not possible to visit the inside of this building as it houses the Presidency of the Assembly of the Communities of Castile-La Mancha.

There are many more façades yet to see. These include the Gothic-Mudejar **Corral de Don Diego** (in Calle Magdalena), which is one of the few remains of the palace of Diego García de Toledo, Lord of Mejorada; the **Palace of Rey Don Pedro** (in the square of the same name), which never in fact belonged to this king but, as demonstrated by the coats of arms dating from the end of the 14th century, to Teresa de Ayala and Fernán Alvárez de Toledo, the Lord and Lady of Higares; the façade of the former palace of the Toledos and Ayalas, which was given in 1477 by María Suárez de Toledo to the **Convent of Santa Isabel** and which is clearly influenced by the Caliphate and magnificently worked; there is the Gothic-Mudejar **Inn of the Brotherhood** (in Calle de la Tripería, very close to the Cathedral), which is decorated with the emblems of the Catholic Monarchs, from the time when the palace was built, and of Philip II flanked by two bowmen of the Holy Brotherhood armed with crossbows. The building was the headquarters and prison of the Holy Brotherhood, an institution which, up until its dissolution at the end of the 18th century, was responsible for ensuring that the fields and roads were safe. The building was then converted into an inn, hence the origin of its name, and it now houses a Municipal Cultural Centre. In addition to the façade, there is a magnificent coffered ceiling in the old court room, as well as part of the cells where criminals were locked up.

Detail of the façade of the Inn of the Brotherhood.

Palace de la Cava and statue of Queen Isabel the Catholic next to the Monastery of San Juan de los Reyes.

Façades of the Palace of Rey Don Pedro and the former palace of the Toledos and Ayalas, which has formed part of the Convent of Santa Isabel la Real since 1447.

Mudejar plasterwork at the Casa de Mesa.

Main façade of the Casa de las Cadenas.　　　*Neo-classical façade in Calle de San Román.*

Here, we have mentioned but a few façades. Evidently, there are many more. Toledo has such a wealth of monuments, history and legends that it is impossible to cover everything, although this itself is one of its charms. Many of these façades are, as we have seen, Gothic-Mudejar and were built when Toledo shone with splendour around the world. However, when Philip decided to move the court to Madrid in 1562, the city began to wane. The fact that it remained the spiritual capital of Spain prevented a more serious decline, with some new buildings even being promoted by the archbishops of Toledo. In spite of this, the palaces were gradually abandoned and over time were converted into blocks of ordinary flats or perhaps demolished. The city barely grew for several centuries, although the space itself of the old centre left little room for major urban changes. In

consequence, we have in Toledo an almost intact medieval city.

But let us continue on our way around old Toledo. There are two further palaces worthy of attention – the **Casa de Mesa** and the **Casa de las Cadenas.** The Casa de Mesa is next to the Church of San Román and is a former palace dating back to the 13th century. Various modifications over time have hidden its original structure but it does still have a beautiful room decorated with lovely Mudejar plasterwork and superb interlaced coffered ceilings. The Casa de las Cadenas in Calle Bulas is a magnificent example of the classic large Toledan house. It is, moreover, one of the easiest houses to visit in the old centre as it holds the **Museum of Contemporary Art,** that was set up in 1975. The three-storey house dates from the 15th century and follows the typical pattern of distri-

Courtyards in Toledo are often decorated with Arab-inspired tiles and ceramics.

bution around a central courtyard. Many of its rooms still have their Mudejar plasterwork and they all have admirable coffered ceilings and wooden roofing.

In general, it is not easy to visit many of these old houses, either because they are privately owned or because they house official bodies. Nevertheless, during the festivities for Corpus Christi, they usually open their doors and reveal their courtyards that are specially decorated for the occasion. Visitors should not, however, expect to find the colourful courtyard full of flowers so typical of Andalusia: the city is essentially introverted and the Toledan courtyard is above all else a place for meditation.

The meandering shady street of **Calle de las Bulas** is one of the most charming in the city. The peace and quiet of some of the alleys in the old centre are surprising after the streets that are nowadays full of tourists and traders, such as Calle de Santo Tomé, Calle de San Juan de la Penitencia, Calle del Comercio and Calle del Hombre de Palo. In contrast with these busy streets, there are some parts of the city where you scarcely hear a soul, perhaps the only noise being the ringing of the bells in a nearby church.

A particularly attractive area of this nature is to be found close to **Plaza de Santo Domingo el Real,** watched over by the monastery of the same name. Here, there are a number of religious communities which turn their austere high walls that have hardly any windows or doors towards us. There are two plaques in the corner of the square that pay homage to Gustavo Adolfo Bécquer, the great Romantic poet who so loved Toledo. Very nearby, in **Calle Buzones**

Three spots in old Toledo: Calle de Santo Tomé, Cuesta de Agustín Moretó and Calle de las Bulas.

The railway station.

heading in the direction of Plaza de San Vicente, are the most characteristic **covered passages** in the city. Built mostly of wood, they are dotted around the entire old centre and were put up to link two buildings belonging to the same owner.

When walking around the city, it is worth paying attention to the names of the streets, many of which evoke old stories. One example is **Calle del Pozo Amargo** –the street of the bitter well– which refers to the story of the beautiful Raquel, who threw herself into a well in the belief that she could see the face of her beloved at the bottom. **Calle de los Alfileritos** was so-called after the old tradition of leaving *alfileres* –pins– for the Virgin in a niche at the start of the street. These were pins which girls had pricked themselves with and they left them for the Virgin in order to ask her for a suitable boyfriend. There is also the **Plazuela de**

Padilla, named after the *comunero* leader Juan de Padilla, who had a house here which Emperor Charles V ordered be burnt and sprinkled with salt «so that grass should never grow there» as an exemplary punishment. The style which has left the deepest mark in Toledo is Mudejar. It is even possible to see the taste for this style in new buildings, such as the **railway station,** which opened in 1920 and which looks like an old Arab palace, with all the detailing: Arab-inspired tiles, plasterwork, etc. In short, there are very few buildings in old Toledo that are clearly of another architectural style. A few examples that might be mentioned are the **Lorenzana Palace,** next to Plaza de San Vicente, which was built at the end of the 18th century on the initiative of Cardinal Lorenzana to house the University, and the **Palace of the Provincial Council,** built in the 19th century on the site of a former monastery

Lorenzana Palace, now the seat of the Rectorate of the University of Toledo.

Palace of the Provincial Council and remains of the ancient walls.

Shrine of the Virgen del Valle and a view of the landing stage next to the Diamond Merchant's House. Here in this beautiful spot on the Tagus is where the boat is kept that is used to take pilgrims over to the other bank of the river and to the path that climbs up to the shrine, although it is now only used for the popular pilgrimage on 1 May.

of the Brothers of Mercy and which was badly destroyed during the French invasion. This palace is next to the **Mirador de la Granja,** the best vantage point with a view over the new part of the city.

For a final look at Toledo, go up to the **Carretera de Circunvalación,** particularly at dusk because twilight is the best moment in Toledo. The ochre colours of the motley of buildings at this time take on a golden hue that gives the city a unique atmosphere. From this road, which follows the sweep of the Tagus River, you can see all of Toledo: the bridges, gates, walls and towers everything in fact. It does not matter where you stop, be it at the vantage point at the **Shrine of the Virgen del Valle** or at the **Conde de Orgaz National Parador** hotel. Along the way you will see a large rambling house surrounded by cypresses and a bit further on a house with olive trees. These are the *cigarrales,* the classic stately country houses typical of Toledo, though many have been recently built or converted into normal places of residence. Their name comes from the cigarra, the cicada whose song is a common feature of nights in these parts. Immortalised by Tirso de Molina in his work *Los Cigarrales de Toledo* (Weekend Retreats of Toledo), perhaps one of the most representative of these buildings is the one at Marañón, where this famous doctor and writer lived.

The cigarral, the traditional Toledan country house, has all the serenity of rural Latin villas.

Corpus Christi: tapestries and a bedecked street.

FESTIVITIES AND POPULAR TRADITIONS

The people of Toledo love the liturgy and ritual. Consequently, they always respect ceremonies, either when they dress up grandly in their finery to attend the Corpus Christi procession or when the go to the spring pilgrimage celebrations. The most important, deeply rooted event is **Corpus Christi,** which falls some time between the end of May and the beginning of June. It has been officially declared as an event of Touristic Interest and is internationally famous. The week before the procession, the streets where it is to pass are protected with awnings and the balconies are decorated with flags, flowers and tapestries, and the Cathedral walls outside are hung with antique tapestries. On the eve, the route is officially opened by a retinue that is preceded by the verger, who uses a bar as high as the Monstrance to check that the awnings are at the right height. At last, the solemn procession begins. Everything draws admiration, from the Monstrance itself to the traditional costumes of the participants and even the floor, which is covered with thyme and rosemary.

In contrast with Corpus Christi, which is a festival of light and colour, **Easter** in Toledo might not enjoy the same fame, but its sobriety is stirring. Also well-known are the **pilgrimages,** the most popular being the pilgrimage of Our Lady of the Valley on 1 May, when the Virgin is taken out on a procession up and down the hills and when the bell at her shrine rings all day because of the tradition that says «the person who does not ring the bell in the valley will not marry». Lastly, there are the **Patronal Festivities** during the week of 15 August in honour of Our Lady of the Tabernacle, when various events are put on and fairground attractions are open.

CRAFTS

Toledo is one of the few cities in the world to have managed to make its local craft internationally prestigious. There is the pottery, damascene work, ironwork, lacemaking and the manufacture of weapons. For centuries, this city on the Tagus has been the site of craftsmen's workshops, which have adopted the knowledge and skills of the various peoples who have passed through it. The most representative of these skilled crafts is unquestionably the art of making swords, although it would be more proper to talk of «Toledan steel» in order to include the fabulous suits of armour that are still made today. A large proportion of production output is sold to tourists, replicas of the famous swords –Tizona, Colada, Boabdil, James I and Excalibur– are all particularly popular. Some manufacturers, nevertheless, continue to make sabres for various armies around the world. This industry was already very active during the time of the Visigoths, although it went into to decline with the emergence of firearms. In 1761, in order to prevent the skill being lost, Charles III founded the Royal Factory of Arms on the outskirts of the old centre in Calle Núñez de Arce, where firearms were also made. It is now possible to watch the skilled process of making swords in a number of workshops scattered around the city. Another related skill is damascene work, a technique which consists in pressing fine metals, especially gold and sil-

Sword and an example of Toledan damascene work.

ver, into steel or metal to form designs or patterns. This was introduced by the Muslims and is used to decorate swords and suits of armour, as well as a whole host of other items, such as plates, jewellery, vases and pins. Various potteries in the province enjoy deserved renown, particularly those of Talavera de la Reina and of El Pueblo del Arzobispo, which have many pieces exhibited as veritable gems in a number of museums around the world. The ceramics of Talavera were already famous by the 16th century. Initially part of the Mudejar tradition, they then turned towards the Renaissance. The classic item from the 16th and 17th centuries is the so-called Tricolor, decorated in blue, orange and manganese. At the end of the 17th and beginning of the 18th centuries, a series called the «Chinesca» (Chinese) or «Golondrinas (Swallows) came to prominence. In these pieces, the main features were the use of pale blue as the colour and of designs of swallows. New shapes of globe pitchers emerged in the middle of the 18th century, as did new, elaborate designs, such as the «Guirnaldas» (Garlands) and «Pabellones» (Pavilions) series. A tremendous variety of colours are now used, but at that time the colours that dominated were the ochre and yellow of the Toledan countryside and the blue of the sky. The most characteristic features of ceramics from El Pueblo del Arzobispo are shades of green and hunting scenes.

Ceramics have a long and noble tradition in Toledo.

One of the best known Toledan sweetmeats is marzipan, which is directly related to Arab confectionery.

GASTRONOMY

Its geographical location between Old Castile, Extremadura and La Mancha means that Toledo offers a rich and varied cuisine. And like all art forms in the region, culinary art in Toledo was influenced by the different cultures that passed through these lands. Broadly speaking, it could be said that the cuisine of Toledo is based essentially on hunting and game: partridges, quail and hares are important elements in the recipes here. Larger game is also highly appreciated, including venison stews. Other main courses that are typical of the region are marinated trout and roast lamb and suckling pig. Starters include pisto manchego (Manchego-style vegetables), tortilla a la magra (tortilla with ham), migas (fried breadcrumbs), gazpacho, Castilian soup and crab soup. For dessert, there is the well-known marzipan, which here is not restricted just to Christmas, and Toledanas stuffed with thin vermicelli. The long tradition in all things to delight a sweet tooth continues with syrup and a wide selection of biscuits and pastries, such as marquesitas, the sugared marzipan cakes called melindres de Yepe, the round rosquillas de Bargas like doughnuts, and many others. The cheeses here also demand serious attention from gourmets. Manchego cheese can be eaten either as an aperitif or after your meal. There are also the pure sheep's milk cheeses and matured cheeses that have been cured in olive oil for over a year. The wines of Toledo are renowned for their robust flavour. There are two *Denominaciones de Origen* (guaranteeing the wine comes from a particular area) in the province. These are La Mancha and Méntrida, with production concentrated mainly in the area of La Mancha.

INDEX

EDITORIAL ESCUDO DE ORO, S.A.
I.S.B.N. 84-378-2029-4
Printed by FISA - Escudo de Oro, S.A.
Dep. Legal B. 31167-2000

Protegemos el bosque; papel procedente de cultivos forestales controlados
Wir schützen den Wald. Papier aus kontrollierten Forsten.
We protect our forests. The paper used comes from controlled forestry plantations
Nous sauvegardons la forêt: papier provenant de cultures forestières contrôlées

ESCUDO DE ORO, S.A. COLLECTIONS

ALL SPAIN

1 MADRID
2 BARCELONA
3 SEVILLE
4 MAJORCA
5 THE COSTA BRAVA
8 CORDOBA
9 GRANADA
10 VALENCIA
11 TOLEDO
12 SANTIAGO
13 IBIZA and Formentera
14 CADIZ and provincia
15 MONTSERRAT
16 CANTABRIA
17 TENERIFE
20 BURGOS
21 ALICANTE
24 SEGOVIA
25 SARAGOSSA
26 SALAMANCA
27 AVILA
28 MINORCA
29 SAN SEBASTIAN and Guipúzcoa
30 ASTURIAS
31 LA CORUNNA and the Rías Altas
32 TARRAGONA
40 CUENCA
41 LEON
42 PONTEVEDRA, VIGO and Rías Bajas
43 RONDA
46 SIGUENZA
47 ANDALUSIA
52 EXTREMADURA
54 MORELLA
58 VALLDEMOSSA

GUIDES

1 MADRID
2 BARCELONA
3 LA RIOJA
4 MAJORCA
6 SANTIAGO DE COMPOSTELA
7 SEVILLA
8 ANDALUCIA
9 GRAN CANARIA
12 GALICIA
13 CORDOBA
14 COSTA BLANCA
15 GRANADA
22 SEGOVIA
25 AVILA
26 HUESCA
28 TOLEDO
30 SANTANDER

---

4 LONDON

---

1 LA HABANA VIEJA
2 EL CAPITOLIO (CUBA)
3 NECROPOLIS DE LA HABANA (CUBA)

ALL EUROPE

1 ANDORRA
2 LISBON
3 LONDON
4 BRUGES
6 MONACO
7 VIENNA
11 VERDUN
12 THE TOWER OF LONDON
13 ANTWERP
14 WESTMINSTER ABBEY
15 THE SPANISH RIDING SCHOOL IN VIENNA
17 WINDSOR CASTLE
18 LA CÔTE D'OPAL
19 COTE D'AZUR
22 BRUSSELS
23 SCHÖNBRUNN PALACE
26 HOFBURG PALACE
27 ALSACE
28 RHODES
32 PERPIGNAN
33 STRASBOURG
34 MADEIRA + PORTO SANTO
35 CERDAGNE - CAPCIR
36 BERLIN
37 MOSCU
38 PORTUGAL

TOURISM

1 COSTA DEL SOL
2 COSTA BRAVA
3 ANDORRA
4 ANTEQUERA
6 MENORCA
8 MALLORCA
9 TENERIFE
14 LA ALPUJARRA
15 LA AXARQUIA
16 PARQUE ARDALES AND EL CHORRO
17 NERJA
18 GAUDI
19 BARCELONA
21 MARBELLA
23 LA MANGA DEL MAR MENOR
25 CATEDRAL DE LEON
26 MONTSERRAT
28 PICASSO
34 RONDA
35 IBIZA-FORMENTERA
37 GIRONA
38 CADIZ
39 ALMERIA
40 SAGRADA FAMILIA
41 FUENGIROLA
42 FATIMA
43 LANZAROTE
44 MEZQUITA HASSAN II
45 JEREZ DE LA FRONTERA
46 PALS
47 VALLDEMOSSA
48 SANTILLANA DEL MAR
49 LA ALHAMBRA Y EL GENERALIFE
51 MONACO-MONTECARLO

ALL AMERICA

1 PUERTO RICO
2 SANTO DOMINGO
3 QUEBEC
4 COSTA RICA
5 CARACAS
6 LA HABANA

---

1 CUZCO
2 AREQUIPA
3 LIMA
4 MACHU PICCHU

ALL AFRICA

1 MOROCCO
3 TUNISIA

ART IN SPAIN

1 PALAU DE LA MUSICA CATALANA
2 GAUDI
3 PRADO MUSEUM I (Spanish Painting)
4 PRADO MUSEUM I (Foreing Painting)
5 MONASTERY OF GUADALUPE
7 THE FINE ARTS MUSUEM OF SEVILLE
10 THE CATHEDRAL OF GIRONA
11 GRAN TEATRO DEL LICEO (Great Opera House)
12 MEZQUITA DE CORDOBA
14 PICASSO
15 ROYAL PALACE OF SEVILLE
19 THE ALHAMBRA AND THE GENERALIFE
21 ROYAL ESTATE OF ARANJUEZ
22 ROYAL ESTATE OF EL PARDO
24 ROYAL PALACE OF SAN ILDEFONSO
26 OUR LADY OF THE PILLAR OF SARAGOSSA
27 TEMPLE DE LA SAGRADA FAMILIA
28 POBLET ABTEI
29 THE CATHEDRAL OF SEVILLE
30 THE CATHEDRAL DE MAJORCA
32 CARTUJA DE VALLDEMOSSA
33 GOYA
34 THE CATHEDRAL OF BARCELONA
35 CASA - MUSEU CASTELL GALA-DALI PUBOL
36 THE CATHEDRAL OF SIGUENZA
37 SANTA MARIA LA REAL DE NAJERA
38 CASA - MUSEU SALVADOR DALI PORT LLIGAT

MONOGRAPHS (S)

5 SOLAR ENERGY IN THE CERDAGNE
10 MORELLA
20 CAPILLA REAL DE GRANADA
31 CORDILLERAS DE PUERTO RICO
38 GIBRALTAR
50 BRUGES
68 MONASTERIO DE PIEDRA
70 TORREVIEJA
74 VALLDEMOSSA
75 ANTWERP
84 CATHEDRAL OF MAJORCA
85 CATHEDRAL OF BARCELONA
86 VALL D'UXO

MONOGRAPHS (L)

5 PUERTO RICO
6 THE OLD SAN JUAN
9 THE CITY OF BRUGES
19 MURALLAS DE SAN JUAN

MAPS

1 MADRID
2 BARCELONA
6 LONDON
8 ALICANTE
20 PANAMA
31 SEVILLE
33 BRUGES
34 BRUSSELS
35 ANTWERP
36 SEGOVIA
37 CORDOBA
38 CADIZ
40 PALMA OF MAJORCA
45 JEREZ DE LA FRONTERA
47 AVILA
48 ANDORRA
50 SALAMANCA
52 LEON
53 BURGOS
58 IBIZA
59 OOSTENDE
78 GRANADA
80 MONACO
93 MENORCA
94 LA MANGA DEL MAR MENOR
96 COSTA BRAVA
97 MADEIRA
98 SANTANDER
99 LLORET DE MAR
100 ANDALUCIA
101 JAEN